SCIENTIFIC AMERICAN EDUCATIONAL PUBLISHING

SCIENTIFIC AMERICAN INVESTIGATES LIFE CYCLES

THE STRANGE LIFE CYCLE OF A CICADA

ANNA MCDOUGAL

Published in 2025 by The Rosen Publishing Group
in association with Scientific American Educational Publishing
2544 Clinton Street, Buffalo NY 14224

Library of Congress Cataloging-in-Publication Data

Names: McDougal, Anna, author.
Title: The strange life cycle of a cicada / Anna McDougal.
Description: Buffalo, NY : Scientific American Educational Publishing, [2025] | Series: Scientific American investigates life cycles | Includes bibliographical references and index.
Identifiers: LCCN 2024008029 (print) | LCCN 2024008030 (ebook) | ISBN 9781725350823 (library binding) | ISBN 9781725350816 (paperback) | ISBN 9781725350830 (ebook)
Subjects: LCSH: Cicadas–Life cycles–Juvenile literature.
Classification: LCC QL527.C5 M423 2025 (print) | LCC QL527.C5 (ebook) | DDC 595.7/52–dc23/eng/20240312
LC record available at https://lccn.loc.gov/2024008029
LC ebook record available at https://lccn.loc.gov/2024008030

Portions of this work were originally authored by Greg Roza and published as *The Bizarre Life Cycle of a Cicada.* All new material in this edition authored by Anna McDougal.

Designer: Tanya Dellaccio Keeney
Editor: Caitie McAneney

Photo credits: Cover SIMON SHIM/Shutterstock.com; p. 5 Achkin/Shutterstock.com; p. 7 (top) EKJYOT SINGH ARORA/Shutterstock.com; p.7 (bottom) Georgi Baird/Shutterstock.com; p. 9 Gerry Bishop/Shutterstock.com; p. 11 Tacio Philip Sansonovski/Shutterstock.com; p. 13 Photour.1904/Shutterstock.com; p. 15 Jamie Noguchi/Shutterstock.com; p. 15 (bottom) aodaodaodaod/Shutterstock.com; p. 17 Grant Heilman Photography/Alamy.com; p. 19 (top) Nyvlt-art/Shutterstock.com; p. 19 (bottom) Eric Isselee/Shutterstock.com; p. 21 wanida tubtawee/Shutterstock.com.

Printed in the United States of America

CPSIA compliance information: Batch #CSSA25. For Further Information contact Rosen Publishing at 1-800-237-9932.

CONTENTS

Words in the glossary appear in **bold** type the first time they are used in the text.

MAKE SOME NOISE

One of the loudest sounds of summer comes from something small. The cicada (suh-KAY-duh) makes a loud buzzing sound. When many cicadas get together, they can really make some noise!

More than 3,000 cicada **species** live on Earth. You can **identify** them by their large oval body and glass-like wings. They have two big eyes with three small eyes between them. They may look a little strange. And their life cycle is even stranger!

Some cicadas sing in such a high **pitch** that humans can't hear them!

FUN FACT

THE WORLD'S LOUDEST INSECT IS THE AFRICAN CICADA. IT CAN GET AS LOUD AS A CHAINSAW!

BUGS WITH BENEFITS

Have you ever seen a cicada? They are big bugs, but they're also great at hiding in trees. You may only hear them. A flying cicada can be a creepy sight! But don't worry—cicadas don't bite.

Cicadas are actually good for people. Many people think cicadas are bad for vegetable crops. However, adult cicadas mainly eat tree sap. Young cicadas dig tunnels in the earth. This lets air into the ground. Then, more plants can grow.

Dead cicadas break down and put important **nutrients** into the soil. They also provide food for many animals.

FUN FACT

CICADAS ARE BIG BUGS. ADULTS CAN BE UP TO 2.25 INCHES (5.7 CM) LONG.

LIFE UNDERGROUND

Cicadas have a long beginning phase of their life cycle. Female cicadas lay eggs on the stems of plants and tree branches. Then, tiny, wingless **larvae** called nymphs break out of the eggs. The nymphs fall to the ground and **burrow** up to 2 feet (61 cm) into the earth.

Nymphs stay alive for years underground by eating sap from tree roots. Some are eaten by beetle larvae before they finish growing up. Some are eaten by birds and wasps. Others continue to grow.

Cicadas **shed** their skin, or molt, several times as they grow. You may find these old skins lying on the ground!

FUN FACT

DEPENDING ON THE SPECIES, THE NYMPHS REMAIN UNDERGROUND FOR 2 TO 17 YEARS.

YOUNG CICADAS

After a number of years, it's time for cicada nymphs to leave the ground. These young cicadas are pale and have a soft **exoskeleton**. Millions of cicadas—called a brood—crawl out of the ground at the same time. In areas where it gets cold in winter, cicadas **emerge** in May when the soil has warmed up.

Young cicadas climb up trees and shed their skin for the last time, becoming adults. Over time, the exoskeleton hardens.

Young cicadas often emerge from underground at night.

FUN FACT

SEVEN SPECIES OF CICADA ARE CALLED PERIODICAL CICADAS. THEY EMERGE AT THE SAME TIME. THE REST, CALLED ANNUAL CICADAS, EMERGE AT DIFFERENT TIMES EACH SUMMER.

ADULT LIFE

Cicadas spend years of their lives as nymphs. However, they live only a very short time as adults. Adult cicadas live up to about 6 weeks. They spend much of this time on trees. Cicadas use a long mouthpart to suck sap out of trees.

Adult cicadas have many predators. These include birds and squirrels. Since so many cicadas emerge in one brood, there's a lot of food for these predators. For those who survive, their main job is to **mate** and lay eggs.

Even after cicadas' predators have eaten their fill, there are still plenty of cicadas left to lay eggs.

WHAT'S THE BUZZ?

When you hear cicadas, you're hearing males "singing." This loud buzzing sound is made to **attract** females. They do this with special parts on their exoskeleton called tymbals. The sound a male makes is a mating call. Females hear the sound and find the males.

All male cicadas in a brood usually produce their mating call at the same time. This can get very loud. Each cicada species has its own special mating call.

The loud song of male cicadas hurts birds' ears. This helps keep them away during mating season.

LAYING EGGS

Female cicadas look for a tree to lay their eggs. They use a sharp spike on their belly to make a cut in a twig. Each female lays 24 to 28 eggs in the cut and moves on to make another cut. This process continues until she has laid all her eggs.

The eggs take four to eight weeks to hatch. Then the cycle will start again. The nymphs will fall to the ground, grow under the earth, and emerge.

FUN FACT

EACH FEMALE CICADA LAYS BETWEEN 200 AND 400 EGGS.

These cicada eggs lie in a nest created in a thin branch.

DIFFERENT BROODS

Different species of cicada spend different amounts of time underground. Some broods spend 17 years underground. Then, billions of these bugs emerge from the earth at once. This gives the species more of a chance to survive because there are so many insects. Predators can't keep up!

Some years, the broods are small and you may not hear them at all. You may not notice cicadas every summer unless you go looking for them.

Some people think cicadas are a **plague** of locusts. However, these insects are different.

CICADA

LOCUST

ALL NOISE

The eastern United States is home to seven species of periodical cicada. Scientists use Roman numerals to keep track of periodical broods. Brood X is the name for a kind of 17-year cicada found in Virginia, Indiana, Tennessee, and Pennsylvania. When Brood X emerges, they can really put on a loud concert!

It can be strange to see so many big bugs flying around at once. However, it's good to remember that they can't hurt you or your pets. They're all noise!

Cicadas spend much longer in the nymph stage of their life cycle than the adult stage.

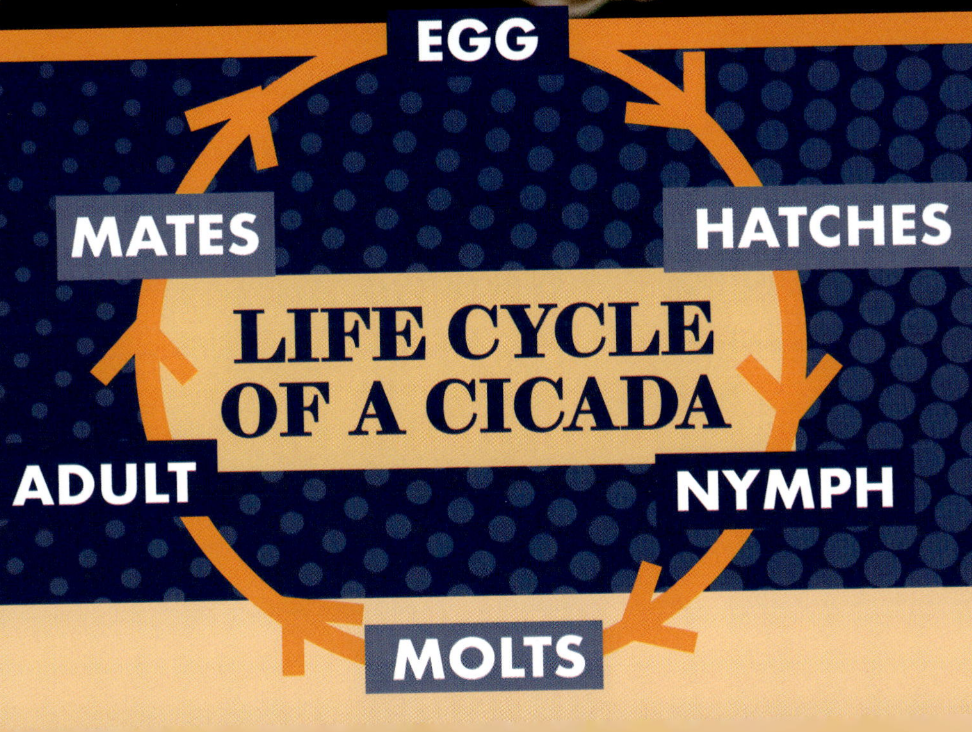

GLOSSARY

attract: To draw toward oneself.

burrow: To tunnel into the ground.

emerge: To come out.

exoskeleton: The hard covering on the outside of an animal's body that holds and guards the soft insides.

identify: To find out the name or features of something.

larvae: Bugs in an early stage of life that have a wormlike form.

mate: To come together to make babies.

nutrient: Something needed for growth and health.

pitch: How high or low a sound is.

plague: A terrible event that harms many people, such as an invasion of harmful insects.

shed: To lose fur, hair, feathers, or skin.

species: A group of animals that are all of the same kind.

FOR MORE INFORMATION

Books

Buller, Laura. *Bugs Hide and Seek.* New York, NY: DK Publishing, 2023.

Fliess, Sue. *Cicada Symphony.* Chicago, IL: Albert Whitman & Company, 2023.

Websites

Cicada

kids.nationalgeographic.com/animals/invertebrates/facts/cicada
Learn exciting facts about cicadas with National Geographic Kids.

Cicadidae

www.biokids.umich.edu/critters/Cicadidae/
Explore questions and answers about cicadas.

Publisher's note to educators and parents: Our editors have carefully reviewed these websites to ensure that they are suitable for students. Many websites change frequently, however, and we cannot guarantee that a site's future contents will continue to meet our high standards of quality and educational value. Be advised that students should be closely supervised whenever they access the internet.

INDEX